5 LESSONS FROM WITTGENSTEIN

Oswald Sobrino, Ph.D.

Sobrino Works

CONTENTS

ABBREVIATIONS AND REFERENCES

Ahmed 2010: Arif Ahmed, "Introduction," in *Wittgenstein's Philosophical Investigations: A Critical Guide*, edited by Arif Ahmed (Cambridge University Press, 2010).

Anscombe 2001: Ludwig Wittgenstein, *Philosophical Investigations*, translated by G. E. M. Anscombe, 3rd edition (Blackwell Publishing, 2001; English and German texts). The central text of Wittgenstein's later philosophy.

BBB 1958: Wittgenstein's *The Blue and Brown Books* published by Blackwell in 1958 after Wittgenstein's death and a source for his later philosophy. Originally dictated to his students.

Eilenberger 2020: Wolfram Eilenberger, *Time of the Magicians: Wittgenstein, Benjamin, Cassirer, Heidegger, and the Decade That Reinvented Philosophy*, translated by Shaun Whiteside (Penguin Books, 2020). Very interesting writer who gives you the cultural and historical context.

Grayling 2001: A. C. Grayling, *Wittgenstein: A Very Short Introduction* (Oxford University Press, 2001).

Hanna 2010: Robert Hanna, "From referentialism to human action: the Augustinian theory of language," pp. 11-29, in *Wittgenstein's Philosophical Investigations: A Critical Guide*, edited by Arif Ahmed (Cambridge University Press, 2010). Advanced and often abstract discussions in this collection of scholarly articles.

Holt 2001: Jim Holt, "Ludwig Has Left the Building," in *The New

York Times Book Review, available at TimesMachine: December 30, 2001 - NYTimes.com, p. 100. Entertaining book review about the clash between Wittgenstein and another famous philosopher, Karl Popper.

Id.: Used to indicate that the citation is exactly the same as the immediately preceding citation (my usage, not that of *The Chicago Manual of Style*); from the Latin for "same" (*idem*).

Kenny 2006: Anthony Kenny, editor, *The Wittgenstein Reader*, 2nd edition (Blackwell Publishing, 2006). A textbook suited for undergraduate courses and for general readers, although it would benefit from some explanatory notes. I take all my quotations of Wittgenstein and all bibliographical information for W's works from this source, unless otherwise indicated.

McDowell 2010: John McDowell, "Are meaning, understanding, etc., definite states?" at pp. 162-78, in *Wittgenstein's Philosophical Investigations: A Critical Guide*, edited by Arif Ahmed (Cambridge University Press, 2010). I was not impressed by this article, but you may differ.

Pears 1977: David Pears, *Ludwig Wittgenstein* (Penguin Books, 1977). Penguin Modern Masters Series.

PG 1969: Wittgenstein's *Philosophical Grammar*, edited by R. Rhees and translated by Anthony Kenny. Published by Basil Blackwell in 1969. Written before the *Philosophical Investigations*.

PI: Wittgenstein's *Philosophical Investigations* published in 1953 after his death. **References to PI refer to Part I followed by section numbers, not page numbers.**

Quinton 2005: Lord Quinton, "Analytic Philosophy," in *The Oxford Guide to Philosophy*, ed. Ted Honderich (Oxford University Press, 2005).

Ryle 1949: Gilbert Ryle, *The Concept of Mind* (Hutchinson's University Library, 1949). See

The Concept of Mind - Google Books.

Schiffer 2005: Stephen Schiffer, "Russell's Theory of Definite Descriptions," in *Mind*, New Series, Vol. 114, No. 456 (Oct., 2005), pp. 1135-1183, available at Russell's Theory of Definite Descriptions (stephenschiffer.com).

Sobrino 2011: my 2011 book *Freedom and Circumstance: Philosophy in Ortega y Gasset*, also available at Amazon.

sic: Latin for "thus," used to note that a quoted awkward or misspelled word or phrase appears this way in the original source.

s.v.: Latin for "under the word"/*sub verbo*. Used to identify an entry in an encyclopedia, guide, or dictionary.

Warnock 2005: Sir Geoffrey Warnock, "Ryle, Gilbert (1900-76)," in *The Oxford Guide to Philosophy*, ed. Ted Honderich (Oxford University Press, 2005).

INTRODUCTION

To write anything on the famous twentieth-century Austrian philosopher of language Ludwig Wittgenstein (1889-1951), who was closely associated with Cambridge University, is a challenge. You cannot read one source about Wittgenstein because, as one authority put it, his "writings are numerous, complicated, and obscure" (Grayling 2001); hence, you must certainly, without any doubt whatsoever, go well beyond my short book. An additional complication is that scholars speak about Wittgenstein's earlier and later philosophies since later in life he rejected as mistaken his famous work *Tractatus Logico-Philosophicus* (1922), although they will point to continuities between the earlier and later philosophies (see Pears 1977, 1; Kenny 2006, Introduction at vii ; Hanna 2010, 12). My short introductory book focuses on his later philosophy as embodied primarily in his *Philosophical Investigations* (1953; henceforth "PI") published after his death, with references at times to other works that are considered precursors to PI. Given the obscurity of Wittgenstein's writings, my commentary is just that: my impressions of what I find valuable today in his often-opaque remarks and sayings. I make no pretense of revealing what was in his head as he wrote. No more and no less. You can find my suggested reading on Wittgenstein in the Abbreviations and References section.

It is also apparent that, in my judgment, Wittgenstein (henceforth often "W") was emotionally unstable. Of course, that biographical detail has no bearing on the objective evaluation of his philosophical views and flashes of insight but is certainly something about which a newcomer to his work should not be kept in the dark. Two unfortunate anecdotes come to mind: his harsh treatment of young pupils when W was a schoolteacher in Austria (Eilenberger 2020, 154); and his allegedly threatening a speaker, the philosopher Karl Popper, at an academic gathering with a fireplace poker (Holt 2001).

So why then bother with Wittgenstein in the face of his obscurity and strange behavior? My answer is his insight on how we should treat and seek to define words. When writing a theological article considering the meaning of the word "bishop" in the New Testament, I was struck with how writers interjected a later, anachronistic definition of the term into the world of the New Testament. It seemed to me that the New Testament gave a sufficiently clear range of meanings to the term "bishop" (in Greek, *episkopos* or overseer) to support the plausibility of the Apostle Peter as the first bishop of Rome (as I maintained). Wittgenstein's idea of language games in which we trace the meaning of a word by looking at its uses in different contexts (as I understood it) appealed to my own instinct that others were inappropriately and naively fastening on one, rigid, and later definition of "bishop" that muddied the question about Peter in an earlier, different context. Wittgenstein and his language games were thus a happy discovery that I found very useful, given the obtuseness of what I had read on the specific issue that I was considering at that time.

So that experience is my reason for viewing Wittgenstein as worthwhile. You will make your own judgment, if you have not done so already. The plan of this book is to consider the following topics from W's later philosophy:

1. Language games (based on W's *Philosophical Grammar*, henceforth "PG," and *Philosophical Investigations*, henceforth "PI");
2. Meaning as use of a word (based on W's *The Blue and Brown Books* anticipating PI; abbreviated as BBB);
3. Thinking and the ghost in the machine (based on PI);
4. Understanding a rule or series (based on PI); and

5. Philosophy as description of language (based on PI).

I quote these works, as needed for critical discussion and commentary, from the selections found in the second edition of Anthony Kenny's well-regarded *The Wittgenstein Reader*. I also reference, as needed for critical discussion, the German text found in the third edition of G. E. M. Anscombe's translation of *Philosophical Investigations* (also used by Kenny in his selections from PI; hereafter "Anscombe 2001"). Note that the *Tractatus Logico-Philosophicus*, containing Wittgenstein's early philosophy, is "the only philosophical work" of Wittgenstein published while he was alive (Kenny 2006, Introduction at vii).

(Minor housekeeping notes: My personal preference is to put block quotations in quotation marks. Unless otherwise stated, italics in a quotation are from the quoted text. I duplicate W's use or non-use of italics in the original German text of PI when quoting a German word from PI.)

Oswald Sobrino, Ph.D.

◆ ◆ ◆

CHAPTER 1 :
LANGUAGE GAMES

I n Kenny's *Wittgenstein Reader*, we see the first mention of language games in an excerpt from Wittgenstein's *Philosophical Grammar* which was written in the nineteen thirties well before the *Philosophical Investigations*, which is the primary work of W's later philosophy (see Grayling 2001, 76). What we find in this excerpt is the transition from a technical logical analysis using the forms of symbolic logic to a discursive, narrative description of the uses of language without the extensive logical apparatus of W's earlier major work the *Tractatus Logico-Philosophicus*. In a way, that was a welcome shift, especially for those of us readers who may have studied but never specialized in symbolic logic.

The excerpt follows:

"Formerly, I myself spoke of a 'complete analysis', and I used to believe that philosophy had to give a definitive dissection of propositions so as to set out clearly all their connections and remove all possibilities of misunderstanding. I spoke as if there was a calculus in which such a dissection would be possible. . . . At the root of all this there was a false and idealized picture of the use of language. . . . instead we must describe a language game related to our own, or rather a whole series of related language games, and it will be in these that such definitions may occur. Such a contrast destroys grammatical prejudices and makes it possible for us to see the use of a word as it really is, instead of *inventing* the use for the word" (Kenny 2006, 37-38, quoting from PG 1969, 210-218; original italics).

I spoke in the introduction of the emotional issues apparently besetting Wittgenstein, but now I must put things in a wider context. What we have read above shows an amazing level of intellectual humility and maturity in which W speaks of his former view of language as false. The anecdotes we read about W indicate someone who was often condescending to the views or intellectual abilities of others. Yet here we glimpse a powerful drive for seeking truth which overcomes any reluctance to admit one's own past errors.

But the shining jewel in his admission of error is his fastening on the language game by which we can "see the use of a word as it really is." This point is what is so fascinating to those of us who have struggled to define words in a specific historical context whether we are dealing with philosophy or biblical studies or other areas in the humanities. The idea of the language game means that the intellectual search for meaning is as messy, as it should be, as the historical contexts of our words and ideas. As noted in the introduction, in my own work, I found it frustrating to read how some in theological studies imposed a later, specific, and restrictive definition of a bishop on an earlier era in which the term had a broader range of meaning. Wittgenstein's embrace of language games was thus a welcome flash of genius freeing scholars from the tyranny of those who latch on to an ahistorical definition that ill fits an earlier and different historical context.

I also found some of that academic definitional tyranny when researching the attitude of the Stoic Seneca to Roman slavery. I often found scholars writing that Stoics did not object to slavery because Stoics were utterly indifferent to one's social circumstances because only virtue counted. This superficial conclusion acted in effect as a knee-jerk definition of Stoicism's view of social and class situations in general. Yet once one took seriously what Stoics really believed about undesirable predicaments such as slavery, this oft-repeated way of defining the Stoic view of slavery collapsed. In contrast, a closer look at how Stoics wrote about slavery as undesirable and as something to be avoided in order to rationally live in accordance with human nature replaced the wrongheaded "definition" with insights from the Stoic language game about slavery and other social circumstances. The simplistic view of Stoics as absolutely indifferent to Roman slavery was replaced by a language game in which Stoics made clear that, however indifferent slavery was when compared to the pursuit of virtue, slavery itself was still undesirable and to be avoided.

Much work in the humanities is about identifying and documenting the language games of other eras that give us a better understanding of the views of others. The abstract definition floating in an ahistorical realm oblivious to context becomes the enemy of authentic historical work in the humanities. Often (but not always) that abstract definition is merely an example of anachronism by which we project our notions from thinkers in a later place and time onto the earlier era that we claim to depict. As I found, the simplistic view of Stoicism and slavery savored more of the influence of Platonism (both before and after the Stoics) than of the Stoics themselves.

As to his rejection of his former views, Wittgenstein described (in a part of the passage that I did not quote) his earlier, erroneous approach to language as resembling the technical work of Bertrand Russell on the grammatical article as a definite description. For those interested in this reference to Russell, I suggest a challenging but interesting article by Stephen Schiffer on that topic (see Schiffer 2005). As you will see, most readers will be grateful that Wittgenstein switched to a different approach.

When we turn to the *Philosophical Investigations* (PI), we are in a different world from that of Russell. Wittgenstein speaks plainly on the notion of language games: "Here the term 'language-game' [Sprach*spiel*] is meant to bring into prominence the fact that the *speaking* of language is part of an activity, or of a form of life" (Kenny 2006, 43, PI, I, 23; German word from Anscombe 2001, 10). He then gives a long list of examples of language games that includes: "Giving orders, and obeying them – Describing the appearance of an object . . . Forming and testing a hypothesis . . . Singing catches . . . Making a joke . . . Asking, thanking, cursing, greeting, praying" (Id.). Everything is included. Now we can breathe in the air of real life as opposed to the rarified atmosphere of symbolic logic.

As part of thinking, we humans define things and ideas. We look for connections in order to advance an analysis, whether in the humanities or in the natural sciences. Wittgenstein describes how we can do this effectively. He speaks naturally about finding something in common among different games:

"Consider for example the proceedings that we call 'games'. I mean board-games, card-games, ball-games, Olympic games, and so on. What is common to them all? – Don't say: 'There *must* be something common, or they would not be called "games" – but *look and see* whether there is anything in common to *all*, but similarities, relationships, and a whole series of them at that. To repeat: don't think, but look!" (Kenny 2006, 44; PI, I, 65-7).

And so we look, and Wittgenstein tells us what we see in a phrase that I find to be his greatest accomplishment:

"I can think of no better expression to characterize these similarities than 'family resemblances' [Familienähnlichkeiten]; for the various resemblances between members of a family: build, features, colour of eyes, gait, temperament, etc. etc. overlap and criss-cross in the same way. – And I shall say: 'games' form a family" (Kenny 2006, 45; PI, I, 65-7; for the German word, see Anscombe 2001, 27 at PI, I, 67).

And that is exactly what many students, scholars, or just plain thinking people do in trying to define an idea. While some fasten to one definition in an arbitrary and selective fashion, others can see that the reality of the language game is not tied to that one arbitrary definition. Thus we end up finding in the evidence of language use the very "family resemblances" that W points out to us. As a result, the thinker who seeks to impose an arbitrary definition on historical language usage is not really thinking at all. Instead of clarifying an idea, his arbitrary definition simply wastes our time. Unfortunately, a lot of academic writing does exactly that: we are given a certain "take" on an issue or idea while failing to look closely at the evidence of the relevant language game.

I have already given examples of that arbitrary fastening on a definition from my own experiences—imposing a later definition of "bishop" on an earlier and different context or mischaracterizing the Stoic view of slavery based on wrongly defining Stoics as absolutely unconcerned with material circumstances. You can likely think of many more such examples in your own specialized research or other life experiences. For example, anyone who has a passing acquaintance with our racial history in the United States knows of the infamous "one-drop rule" that defined as black any person with a traceable amount of black ancestry. This definition was obviously part of the evil system of enslavement and the later malicious Jim Crow system of segregation. Yet the definition somehow persists in North American culture; while other cultures, such as those in Latin America, find such a definition absurd. These two cultures have two very different language games attempting to define racial identity. Wittgenstein alerted us to look and see the malleability of the act of defining by seeing the language game for what it really is. That contribution is the mark of genius as shown by how Wittgenstein's work is relevant to so many different fields of inquiry far beyond his own specialty in the philosophy of language.

CHAPTER 2: MEANING AS USE OF A WORD

This short chapter further fleshes out how words have meaning in a language game based on Wittgenstein's work in the *Blue and Brown Books* prior to *Philosophical Investigations*. The odd name "Blue and Brown Books" arose because W dictated to his students the books' contents which were then bound in these colors for distribution before eventual publication to a general audience (see Grayling 2001, 76, 78). He anticipates the language games described in *Philosophical Investigations*:

"Think of words as instruments characterized by their use, and then think of the use of a hammer, the use of a chisel, the use of a square, of a glue pot, and of the glue. . . . We are inclined to forget that it is the particular use of a word only which gives the word its meaning. Let us think of our old example for the use of words: Someone is sent to the grocer with a slip of paper with the words 'five apples' written on it. The use of the word *in practice* is its meaning. . . . [A] label would only have a meaning to us in so far as we made a particular use of it" (Kenny 2006, 189, 191; BBB 1958, 66-70).

W refers to an earlier example concerning apples:

"Let us look at a simple example of operating with words. I give someone the order: 'fetch me six apples from the grocer', and I will describe a way of making use of such an order: The words 'six apples' are written on a bit of paper, the paper is handed to the grocer, the grocer compares the word 'apple' with labels on different shelves. He finds it to agree with one of the labels, counts from 1 to the number written on the slip of paper, and for every number counted takes a fruit off the shelf and puts it in a bag. – And here you have *one* use of words. I shall in the future again and again draw your attention to what I shall call language games. These are ways of using signs simpler than those in which we use the signs of our highly complicated everyday language" (Kenny 2006, 42; BBB 1958, 16-17).

This simple example and other similarly simple examples can grant us insight to more complex uses of words. The key is to take the complex use and find how it is being used in a particular language game.

I go back to my own example from church history on defining a "bishop." Writers will state or just assume that a bishop is what students of church history call a monarchical bishop, namely, one and only one supreme overseer of church affairs in a particular place. Yet, we see in the New Testament a more complex and fluid picture: we see many elders or presbyters who seem to be synonymous with bishops (overseers). So who then is *the* bishop? The question is nonsensical in the setting of the earliest forms of Christianity. Thus, in ancient Rome, the early Christian community likely had several or many presbyter-bishops. In that early language game, the term "bishop" did not mean one and only one supreme authority but a group sharing authority in various churches (or, better, house churches) in a particular city. If then an apostle, one of those who accompanied the earthly Jesus or had a recognized encounter with the risen Jesus, arrives in a particular city, he also is obviously an overseer and an authoritative elder, i.e., he is a presbyter-bishop like several others. If this apostle remains in that city for a significant period, then clearly he would become the most important of the presbyter-bishops. Eventually, after a time, he would be viewed as *the* eminent bishop or overseer of all the Christian gatherings in that particular city. That is how my own research concluded that it is historically plausible that Peter became the first "bishop" of Rome: the first of the presbyter-bishops to acquire precedence over the other presbyter-bishops.

The language game requires defining the context—what German scholars in biblical studies call the *Sitz im leben* ("situation in life"). The use or meaning of "bishop" arises from the *Sitz im leben*, the living context of that period in history. To take "bishop" as meaning only the monarch (i.e., the sole overseer) of a particular city full of Christian communities is true only in a different language game from a later period in history. If we mix up or ignore the different language games, then we create confusion, argument, and bickering over words. Focusing on the language game evaporates the verbal conflicts. We can then look for what is common among the different language games—what W calls the family resemblances. In my particular example, the family resemblances fasten on defining "bishop" as an apostle or a successor of an apostle: the person who becomes the preeminent overseer, as the apostles were, in a specifically defined physical area even if in very early times the label "bishop" was not exclusive to him alone.

Wittgenstein's previously quoted rule of thumb is well-taken: "don't think, but look" (see Ch. 1). He is not urging us to suspend reasoning, but rather to look before starting a long chain of reasoning based on abstract notions of what a word must mean and so warns us that "what makes it difficult for us to take this line of investigation is our craving for generality" (Kenny 2006, 43; BBB 1958, 16-17). What W recommends is an empirical approach which is what the best work in the humanities and especially in the history of institutions or ideas is. In the history of philosophy, for example, there is a long chain of ideas and debates about what constitutes knowledge (epistemology). Each philosopher in that debate initiates his answer by assuming or proposing a particular language game. The next philosopher in line proposes a different language game and so the definition of "knowledge" changes. Much of the history of Western philosophy is studying these successive language games on epistemology and other topics.

W's emphasis on the use of words is very close to what the American pragmatist philosophers, such as William James and John Dewey, viewed as truth: what works and persists in working pragmatically in our environment becomes true. The Spanish existentialist philosopher José Ortega y Gasset also proposes a pragmatic view of meaning and truth: my interaction with my particular circumstance in my life. There is a convergence between Wittgenstein, the American pragmatist philosophers, and Ortega y Gasset: look at the use and function in life of our words before settling on (or, as W would say, "inventing," as noted in Ch. 1) an abstract, unchanging definition. Interestingly, Wittgenstein defines a language game as reflecting a "Lebensform/life-form" (Anscombe 2001, 10, at PI, I, 23) and so reminds me especially of Ortega's emphasis on life as the framework for all philosophy.

◆ ◆ ◆

CHAPTER 3: THINKING AND THE GHOST IN THE MACHINE

When Wittgenstein writes in *Philosophical Investigations* about thinking, as discussed in this chapter, I am reminded of the popular philosophical phrase "Ghost in the Machine." The phrase comes from a famous 1949 book *The Concept of Mind* by Oxford philosopher Gilbert Ryle (see Warnock 2005 s.v. "Ryle, Gilbert (1900-76)"). In that book, Ryle refers to Descartes' well-known mind-body dualism as depicting the mind, in Warnock's words, "as a ghostly counterpart of the body, a non-physical 'thing' mysteriously present 'in' the physical body, and the scene or agent of non-physical states, happenings, and acts," and thus as the "ghost in the machine" (Id.). Whether Wittgenstein influenced Ryle is unclear, although A. C. Grayling does not see any significant Wittgenstein influence on Ryle (Grayling 2001, 128-29). Interestingly, Grayling does not comment on whether Ryle influenced Wittgenstein although one naturally thinks of Ryle when reading some of Wittgenstein's writings.

Turning back to Ryle's critique of Descartes, we note that poor Descartes was also the target of many other twentieth-century philosophers for the failure of his dualism to reflect lived experience. My own preference among these critiques is that of the existentialist philosopher José Ortega y Gasset (1883-1955) who emphasized that Descartes placed the "I" of his famous "I think therefore I am"/*Cogito ergo sum* in a falsely privileged position that denied the ultimate and basic reality of human life **within which** the "I" coexists with its circumstance (Sobrino 2011, Chapter 4).

Despite my preference for Ortega's approach to Descartes, Ryle's "ghost in the machine" (Ryle 1949) is so memorable a phrase that I cannot help but recall it as I read Wittgenstein on thinking:

"Now if it were asked: 'Do you have the thought before finding the expression?' what would one have to reply? And what, to the question: 'What did the though consist in, as it existed before its expression?' This case is similar to the one in which someone imagines that one could not think a sentence with the remarkable word order of German or Latin just as it stands. One first has to think it, and then one arranges the words in that queer order. . . . But didn't I already intend the whole construction of the sentence (for example) at its beginning? So surely it already existed in my mind before I said it out loud! If it was in my mind, still it would not normally be there in some different word order. But here we are constructing a misleading picture of 'intending', that is, of the use of this word. An intention is embedded in its situation, in human customs and institutions. . . . In so far as I do intend the construction of a sentence in advance, that is made possible by the fact that I speak the language in question. . . . . Thinking is not an incorporeal process which lends life and sense to speaking, and which it would be possible to detach from speaking . . . . One cannot guess how a word functions. One has to *look* at its use and learn from that" (Kenny 2006, 124-25; PI, I, 316-49).

For Wittgenstein, as I understand him (he is not easy to follow, as is generally acknowledged), one cannot think in language without knowing the language. The already familiar language game is in the thinking. Thus, W calls us to recognize the inescapable nature of looking at language games. Looking at the games is what tells us what someone was intending when the person said this or that.

As I articulate W's point, I find confirmation in the way we evaluate someone's account, for example, of a person trying to explain their conduct in a specific encounter with another person. For my illustration, I assume the context of an American jury trial based on my experiences as a former attorney. The person (let us assume a trial witness under examination) testifies that they lied to another person when they expressed a favorable view of some ongoing or proposed illegal activity. The jury finds that testimony suspect because the expression of consent to the illegal activity was stated in language that the jurors recognize as whole-hearted and even enthusiastic. (Let's assume that both the testifying witness and the jurors share the same native language and so are in the same intuitive language game.) Yet the witness persists in denying at any time genuine consent to the illegal activity.

The jurors then, as usual, must weigh credibility. On the one hand, the witness is lying to us because the witness fears the repercussions from our verdict. Or the witness is being truthful, and we must find some duress present when he spoke the ostensible consent. If the jurors do not find any element of duress, then the jurors are stuck. The jurors must now postulate that the witness suffers some personality defect or quirk that makes the witness such a people-pleaser that the witness habitually expresses enthusiasm for what he intends, all along, to reject.

The attorney for the witness then points to subsequent language used by the witness to reject the illegal plans of the other person. That subsequent language, the lawyer argues, was emphatic in tone and led the other person to depart forthwith. Now the jurors are looking, as W always urges, at the entire pertinent language game *in this situation* and may reasonably conclude that the witness's testimony that his initial consent was a lie is, after all, credible due to his subsequent conduct.

Thus, the solution was not found in speculating about the inexhaustible psychological inner world of the witness but rather by looking at all the language used by the witness. The jurors may feel that the witness suffers from an excessive co-dependence that leads the witness to habitually say untrue things, without duress, so as not to ruffle the feathers of others (hence the jurors may not wish to have someone like the witness as a friend or partner in their personal lives). But the jurors are not contemplating a personal relationship with the witness. The jurors are not psychologists and have no time for psychoanalysis. The jurors must make a practical judgment using common sense, as the trial judge will instruct them to do. The only way out of the quandary of credibility is to look at the language game as a whole in this particular situation and reasonably conclude that the witness, however psychologically strange, did in fact stupidly lie when he initially consented to the proposed illegal plan.

The example of the trial witness illustrates that we discover what one is thinking, one's intent, by look at the full situational language game in particular circumstances. Jurors do it all the time. So do the rest of us in ordinary life when we act prudently. In the humanities, we caution ourselves not to take a certain phrase or sentence out of context. We need the context to make a sound judgment of what, in an example from my research, the philosopher Seneca or St. Paul thought about Roman slavery. The language game provides the context. In religious matters, the ignoring of the language game is notorious. One sect quotes out of context one verse from the Bible as definitive; another sect, disagreeing, simply quotes a different verse out of context. And so, to borrow from St. Paul, they devour each other. Of course, we can find secular parallels to this mutual devouring.

The goal of clarity by looking at language is not unique to Wittgenstein but is present in other contemporary philosophers such as Gilbert Ryle who sought to diffuse our philosophical confusions by clarifying our use of language. Is there a ghost in the machine? All that I would say is that, if there is a ghost in the machine, it makes no difference in the search for meaning. Thought and intention are detectible from looking closely and thoroughly at the relevant language game. Searching for any ghost in the machine becomes unnecessary.

Here is the value of Wittgenstein's insights: they simplify our method of inquiry in many areas, not just in philosophy. I have mentioned examples from history (Seneca and Paul on Roman slavery) and described in detail one hypothetical but realistic scenario from the legal world. The best way to check on the value of W's insights is to consult your own experiences and look closely at the language games involved.

CHAPTER 4:
UNDERSTANDING A
RULE OR SERIES

In various pages of his *Philosophical Investigations*, Wittgenstein goes on and on about a particular language game: "A gives an order [that] B has to write down [a] series of signs according to a certain formation rule" (Kenny 2006, 99; PI, I, 143). W then explores what we mean when B says that he understands this formation rule. What is of interest to me is how W explains understanding as something that is not a mental process as in the phrase "the ghost in the machine." In the ensuing pages (Kenny 2006, 99-103; PI, I, 145-155), W gives the example of teaching B to write down a series of numbers and then to learn to continue that same series and asks what does it mean to say that B has understood the series. Then W switches the example slightly: B observes A write down a series of numbers, and B then discovers how to continue the series: "If he succeeds he exclaims: 'Now I can go on!' " (Kenny 2006, 101; PI, I, 145-55).

W then proposes various possible meanings for B's being able to go on with the series of numbers whether by understanding a formula or in some other way. W points out that "[w]e are trying to get hold of the mental process of understanding" without much success because the task is so slippery (Kenny 2006, 102; PI, I,

145-55). In the end, Wittgenstein tells us:

"Try not to think of understanding as a 'mental process' at all. – For *that* is the expression which confuses you. But ask yourself: 'in what sort of case, in what kind of circumstances' do we say, 'Now I know how to go on,' when, that is, the formula *has* occurred to me? . . . . for us it is *the circumstances* under which he had such an experience that justify him in saying in such a case that he understands, that he knows how to go on" (Kenny 2006, 102-103; PI, I, 145-55).

W pursues a discussion that is not easy to follow. In the end, he concludes: do not search for mental processes, but look at the circumstances of B's experience in understanding the number series.

What can we make of W's investigation? I take this lesson. Others may take other lessons (it seems that the issue about following a rule has generated a lot of ink in Wittgenstein studies). What I see is W warning us that, regardless of how an individual chooses to describe his own experience of understanding, what we are doing as observers of his understanding is focusing on his experiences. We do not assume the ghost in the machine and so impose a particular predetermined solution to the question of B's understanding of the rule behind the number series. We look at the circumstances.

Circumstances are not optional. Everything we do or are takes place, as Ortega y Gasset says, in our coexistence with our circumstance. That coexistence is the focus, not searching for mental processes inside B. I admit that I am an admirer of the philosophy of Ortega y Gasset and that admiration may lead me to impose his framework on what Wittgenstein is saying. Yet, it is fair for me to look at W's words and report the connections I see with Ortega's framework of "I am I and my circumstance" (see Sobrino 2011, Chapter 4, on this Ortega quote). The connection between Wittgenstein and Ortega is that my understanding cannot be separated from my circumstances. W's discussion leads to the same point made by Ortega, whether W in fact shared Ortega's view of ultimate reality as coexistence with my circumstance or whether W would approve of my interpretation.

The answer then, in my view, of how B understands how to continue the number series is based on the circumstances B reports. As W points out, B could have been thinking of a formula or not thinking of a formula. How B understands depends on how B chooses to attack the challenge of understanding the number series—how B chooses to interact with the circumstance in which this challenge takes place.

My own example is more concrete than trying to continue a number series. Let's assume a physical problem or challenge as might occur to a carpenter, a mechanic, or just an ordinary homeowner: how do I repair something. The thing to be repaired poses a challenge as the number series did: how do I get the thing to continue to function. One person may seek to find out what part can repair the problem. If the homeowner is trying to seal a winter draft in the doorway, he can go in several directions in understanding how to repair the draft. He could on the one hand focus on the measurements of the door and seek to replace the door so that the door is now fitting in an airtight fashion. Or the homeowner could prescind from the idea of changing the door itself and focus on plugging the gap which allows the air to enter the house. How then has each homeowner understood the problem posed by the repair challenge? One focuses on replacing the door, the other on plugging the gap. Both solutions can succeed. Upon the success of either solution, we can say that the homeowner did indeed understand the challenge as proven by the successful repair outcome.

What does this prosaic example of the troublesome door tell us about what we mean by understanding something? I propose that understanding something is being able to implement a solution or repair to keep that something "going" just as Wittgenstein posed the challenge of keeping the numerical series going. But the understanding is not reducible to one formula or one approach. The understanding is shaped by the particular circumstances and how the homeowner chose to interact with those circumstances. One chose to focus on changing the door, the other chose to focus on closing the gap between the door and the house. Here we have a pragmatic view of understanding: what works to keep the door going on as an effective door into winter is equivalent to understanding the challenge. (The situation is similar to two physicians curing an ailment with two different approaches— both understood the ailment despite their different responses.) Thus there is no one understanding that can be imposed on the problem. B interacting in his own peculiar way with the challenge defines the understanding. The language game of understanding and knowledge is thus inherently circumstantial which seems to me to be, after all, the quintessential mark of Wittgenstein's conception of a language game.

Wittgenstein was a talented engineer, architect, logician, and mathematician. The abstract (and difficult) nature of his discussion of understanding is thus not surprising. Since I do not fit into any of those categories, my humble description of repairing the door helps me to understand something that I find useful in Wittgenstein's discussion: understanding arises from our interaction with our circumstance and that understanding is correct (not necessarily exclusively correct) when it repairs the challenge posed by my troublesome circumstance.

(For those interested in a more specialized discussion of Wittgenstein on following a rule, see McDowell 2010; warning: I was not impressed by the McDowell discussion.)

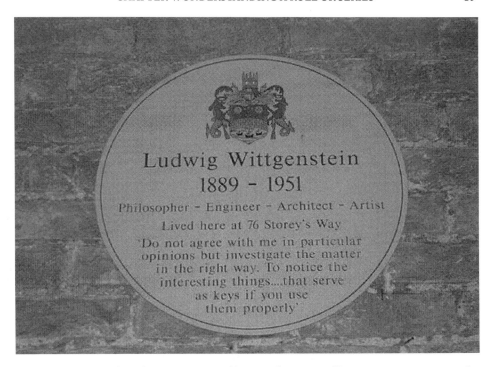

Plaque in Cambridge, U.K. Credit: Andreas Kolbe, CC BY-SA 3.0, via Wikimedia Commons

♦ ♦ ♦

CHAPTER 5:
PHILOSOPHY AS
DESCRIPTION OF
LANGUAGE

The remarks that I choose to illustrate Wittgenstein's view of the task of philosophy are blessedly clearer than some other remarks that we have already seen in this book. Nevertheless his view of philosophy is still unsettling because it seeks to contradict the way that many in the West have viewed philosophy in previous eras as disclosing new knowledge about the world (metaphysics) and about how to live (ethics). Yet what W proposes is not so much that philosophy does not contribute new knowledge as that what we *think* is new knowledge is merely a reminder of what was already known in some sense but about which we were confused—similar to the justification for Socratic teaching methods. This view of philosophy has played a role in the history of what is called Anglo-American analytic philosophy (see Quinton 2005 s.v. "Analytic Philosophy").

Let us consider Wittgenstein on philosophy in the *Philosophical Investigations*:

"We must do away with all *explanation*, and description alone must take its place. And this description gets its light, that is to say its purpose, from the philosophical problems. These are, of course, not empirical problems; they are solved, rather, by looking into the workings of our language, and that in such a way as to make us recognize those workings: *in despite of* [sic] an urge to misunderstand them. The problems are solved, not by giving new information, but by arranging what we have always known. Philosophy is a battle against the bewitchment of our intelligence by means of language" (Kenny 2006, 250; PI, I, 109).

This appears to me to be a very workable and wise definition of philosophy although I do not take it in the radical sense, that W apparently intended, of overturning all previous ways of philosophizing. The powers of human reason allow us to clarify our understanding of ourselves, our world, and our morality. Those powers work by persuasion that reveals to someone a neglected or forgotten aspect of reality. The persuaded reader or listener assents to that revelation because he or she finds it reasonable, coherent, and congruent with personal experience. The persuaded recover from their amnesia.

What I do take as radical in W's view of philosophy is methodological: we must pay very close attention to our language games so that we avoid confusion, avoid the conflation of different terms from different language games, and avoid ignoring that the same term can mean different things in different language games, some of which are contemporaneous and some of which are earlier or later in time. As I have noted from my own research, we can often undermine a certain intellectual agenda or an unexamined intellectual prejudice when we examine the language game being played and compare it to other language games. Attention to the various sense of our words and distinguishing those senses have been the hallmark of Western philosophical writing for centuries. In my opinion, Wittgenstein's genius has not changed that at all; but Wittgenstein has refocused our concern on taking great care to examine the language games which populate the way in which we speak about beliefs, ethics, and the work of other thinkers. It seems to me that Wittgenstein's ghost lurks, to our great benefit, every time a careful researcher corrects others' neglect of language games.

◆ ◆ ◆

CONCLUDING REFLECTION: A "THANK YOU" TO WITTGENSTEIN

When I have written about other thinkers, I have felt that I stood on firm ground in drawing general conclusions as backed by the texts that they had written. But Ludwig Wittgenstein's writings are at times so odd, so terse, and obscure that I am compelled to emphasize that my commentary is my personal reaction to his work and how I make use of his insights as I understand them. It seems that this challenging experience is not mine alone. One Wittgenstein expert from Cambridge University notes that "in the later work Wittgenstein jumps from one topic to another in ways that do not always exhibit any very evident logical connection" (Ahmed 2010, 3). The same scholar confirms how W is thus subject to conflicting interpretations: "Wittgenstein's famous discussion of rule-following has received such fundamentally opposing interpretations that it is hard to characterize its drift in anything approaching neutral terms" (Ahmed 2010, 7).

So, in concluding, I share with you how I use Wittgenstein in my own thinking and writing. When I approach a text from the past, as in my field of Roman studies, I consider the original language, read the comments of others, and apply my own independent insights and synthesis based on my own, hopefully broad and deep, reading and study of the ancient world. How does Wittgenstein help me in this task?

First, Wittgenstein makes me suspect the often overly emphatic conclusions of even highly reputable scholars who assume certain definitions when discussing the intent and beliefs of an ancient figure such as, for example, Seneca the Younger. That healthy suspicion is based on going back to the primary sources themselves and evaluating such scholarly assumptions by what the ancient writer himself wrote rather than on what a chain of modern critical scholars have assumed as obvious. Wittgenstein began his philosophical career working with the famous Bertrand Russell. The later Wittgenstein turned his back on that initial project—an act that points to Wittgenstein's intellectual humility despite his personal shortcomings. No scholar is too famous to be enmeshed in a wrongheaded approach—even Bertrand Russell with his formidable skill and creativity as a logician.

Second, Wittgenstein makes me suspect those who do not explicitly define their central terms by examining the language games present in our primary sources. All definitions arise from a particular language game. Intellectual hygiene requires that we describe that language game for the reader or the student sitting in a lecture hall. Often historians fail to realize that their work requires the philosophical task of clarifying the language game through which they present an historical event or issue. In this sense, every historian must play the role of a linguistic philosopher at the beginning of her writing. I have not seen much of that in historical writing. Often the historian jumps headlong into summarizing past events and making authoritative judgments without first describing the language game that he proposes, as if the sources speak without complication for themselves when in fact each document is part of an intentional language game. That is why, for example, Julius Caesar can be an outright villain engaged in genocide to some but a misunderstood pioneering reformer to others; and Augustus can be a bloodthirsty totalitarian or an amiable and shrewd author of peace and stability.

Thus I use Wittgenstein to describe the relevant historical language game and the role various terms play in that historical game. Textual evidence serves to illuminate what language game the historical figure is playing rather than our naively assuming that the text is simply a picture of historical reality (analogous to Wittgenstein's early view of language as pictorial, which he ultimately rejected; see Grayling 2001, 78-79). Critics will inevitably dispute the use and description of a particular language game by a historian, but at least we will know what we are disputing instead of simply offering the public contradictory portraits without pointing out the bases of those contradictions. For that contribution, I feel a certain profound gratitude toward Ludwig Wittgenstein.

ABOUT THE AUTHOR

Oswald Sobrino

Oswald Sobrino holds a Ph.D. in Latin and Roman Studies (University of Florida) and has taught at the college level for many years.

Made in the USA
Columbia, SC
29 October 2022

70149013R00022